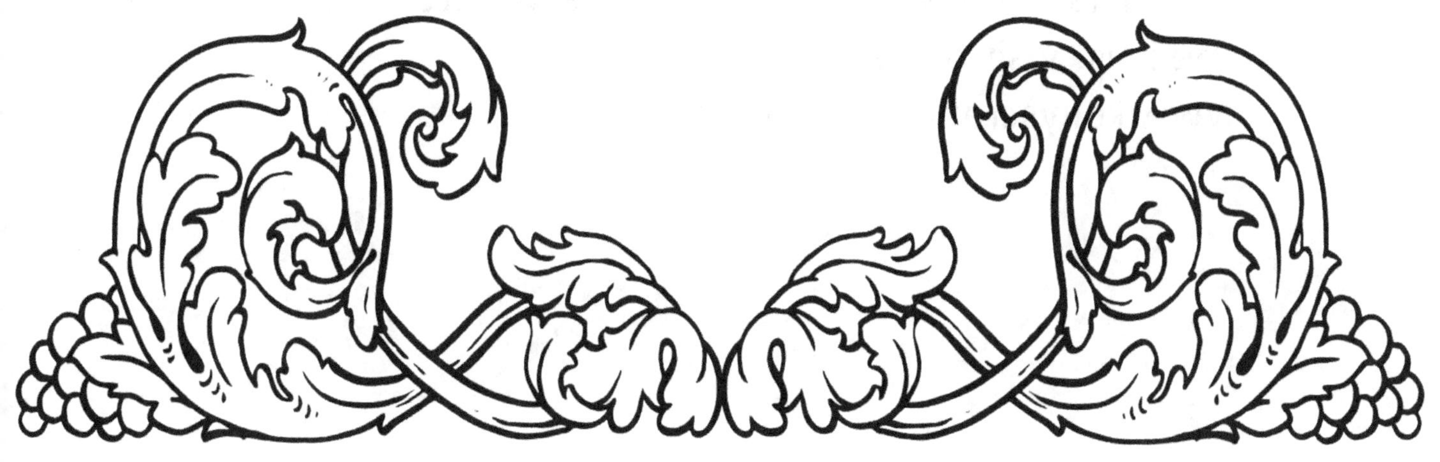

VINTAGE LADIES

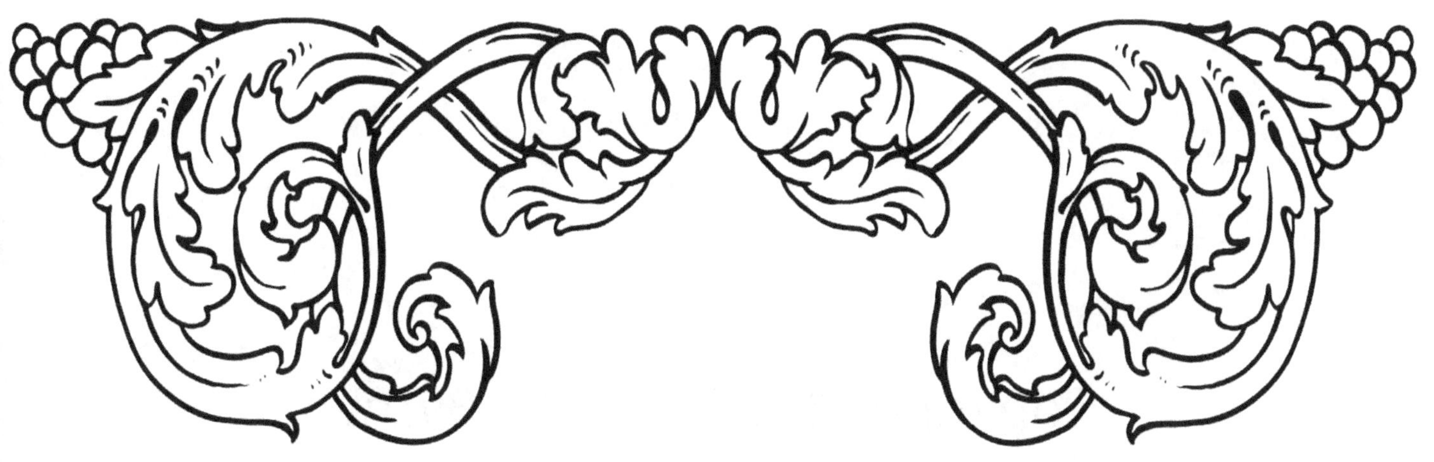

Kelly's Crafty Corner has a range of journals, notebooks, colouring books and other craft. Sign up to our newsletter to keep up to date with new products and specials as well as newsletter only specials. Visit our website at: www.kellyscraftycorner.com